Coffee With Jesus
The Second Cup

by Todd Uebele

"During our walk with Christ, we will all go through peaks and valleys. The important thing is to keep walking."

Coffee With Jesus, the 2nd Cup
By Todd Uebele

ISBN 13: 978-1-7341693-1-7

Scripture taken from the HOLY BIBLE, New International Version (NIV) Copyright © 1973, 1978, 1984 by International Bible Society. Used by permission of Zondervan Bible Publishers.

Quote from Week 4, Day 6, courtesy of Aaron Burks. Used with permission.

Week 1, Day 7, written by Richard "Rick" Schuette. Used with permission.

Week 3, Day 7, written by Elizabeth Bristol, based off of her book, "Marry Me: One Woman's Incredible Adventure with God." Used with permission.

All other written material is the original work of Todd Uebele, Copyright © 2012-2025, all rights reserved. Material may be quoted/used for personal or group teaching only. Material may not be published, reproduced or used in any way for sale, profit or other means except for those listed above. For specific permission of use, contact the publisher for written permission.

One Body Press
info@onebodypress.org

One Body Press
www.onebodypress.org
info@onebodypress.org

TABLE OF CONTENTS

PREFACE vii
Week 1: Character 1
    Day One: Are You Recognizable? 3
    Day Two: Good Fizbar! 4
    Day Three: God's Sabbath Rest 5
    Day Four: A Light in the Darkness 6
    Day Five: It Starts With Us 7
    Day Six: No Limits 8
    Day Seven: Reeling in Serenity 9
    Week 1 Notes 10
Week 2: Reflections 13
    Day One: Reflections on Lent 15
    Day Two: Reflections on Growth 16
    Day Three: Reflections on Rain 17
    Day Four: Reflections on Scars 18
    Day Five: Reflections on Worship 19
    Day Six: Reflections On Revenge 20
    Day Seven: Reflections on Holidays 21
    Week 2 Notes 22
Week 3: Comfort 25
    Day One: Help You Find Your Way 27
    Day Two: God is With Us 28
    Day Three: God is in the Details 29
    Day Four: It's ok to Fail 30
    Day Five: Driving Through Rainbows 31
    Day Six: Fly Away Free 32
    Day Seven: Have You Ever Danced with God? 33
    Week 3 Notes 34

Week 4: God Is 37
    Day One: Our Refuge 39
    Day Two: Our Protector 40
    Day Three: Our Strength 41
    Day Four: Our Deliverer 42
    Day Five: Our Healer 43
    Day Six: Our Helper 44
    Day Seven: Our Comforter 45
    Week 4 Notes 45

Week 5: Recovery 49
    Day One: Give It to God 51
    Day Two: Talk to God 52
    Day Three: Read God's Word 53
    Day Four: Listen to God 54
    Day Five: Perseverance 55
    Day Six: Spread Hope 56
    Day Seven: Spread Comfort 57
    Week 5 Notes 58

Week 6: Above and Beyond 61
    Day One: Beyond Hate 63
    Day Two: Beyond Death 64
    Day Three: Beyond Moving 65
    Day Four: The Cat Came Back 66
    Day Five: Beyond College 1 67
    Day Six: Beyond College 2 68
    Day Seven: Beyond Victory 69
    Week 6 Notes 70

Week 7: Give it to God 73
    Day One: Coffee to Calm the Nerves 75
    Day Two: How to Recover From Rock Bottom 76

Day Three: The Bear 77

Day Four: Gorilla Tape.. 78

Day Five: Is it OK to be Anxious? 79

Day Six: God's Got This..80

Day Seven: Who are You? 81

Week 7 Notes.. 82

Week 8: You Are a Child of God 85

Day One: God of Comfort 87

Day Two: Be Like a Child.. 88

Day Three: Will God Forgive Me?... 89

Day Four: Will God Restore Me? 90

Day Five: God of Second Chances... 91

Day Six: Did We Miss the Rapture?.. 92

Day Seven: You Matter!.. 93

Week 8 Notes.. 94

ACKNOWLEDGEMENTS

There are several people with whom this would not have been possible. I would be remiss if I did not thank them and acknowledge the help, encouragement and support they have given me.

First, I would like to thank Stacee, who has stood by me, supported me and encouraged me, even when progress was slow. This book was finished in no small part due to her love and support.

I would also like to thank contributors: Elizabeth and Rick. This book is much better with your contributions!

I would also like to thank my beta readers: Sara, Leanne, Sarah T., Yilda, and my outstanding editor, Brad. Your input has made this book so much better!

PREFACE

I love writing, and I love observing. For me, writing is a way to record my observations and insights as reminders of what is important. During my deployments to Afghanistan and Qatar, I had both successes and failures in my spiritual life and keeping a record of my thoughts helped me to maintain a positive outlook

There were times where my walk with Jesus was at a peak. There were other times when my walk was deep in the valley. Writing helped me remember the times at the peak in order to help me get through the valleys. It also helped me remember the valleys, so I could value my time at the peak.

Some of what you read here will be about my failures; those times I was in the valleys. Some of what you read will be from the peaks. I am sharing both here in the hope that you can relate, soldier on through the valleys and value your time at the peak.

During our walk with Christ, we will all go through peaks and valleys. The important thing is to keep walking.

TRU

Introduction: Why This Book?

Shortly after "Coffee With Jesus" was published, I was having breakfast with a ministry partner. We were talking about the new book and what was next. I mentioned that I felt the Lord was leading me to write another book, but I needed to pray about it and confirm that was what He was calling me to do.

At the end of our breakfast, she leaned forward and said, "You don't need to pray about it anymore. You know what you need to do. God has already told you. Now, it's time for you to listen."

I was blown away, and I did start this devotional shortly after that breakfast conversation. Since then, so much has changed in the world. This book sat unfinished for a long time, but as the hunger for comfort became more and more apparent, I realized that the time had come to finish it.

This devotional is written to help you in your spiritual walk. It is also written to bring you comfort and hope.

Each week is immediately followed by a short section where you can take notes. It is my hope that you will be able to relate to the devotionals and learn from them. The notes sections are there for you to record your own observations and insights.

I had tossed around the idea of adding questions or prompts but ultimately decided against it. Some of the devotionals will ask questions or give you certain topics to think about, but the notes section is your canvas.

I decided to give you a blank canvas so you can record whatever thoughts or reflections you have. This is your journey, and I am so glad you chose this book to accompany you. It is my hope that you will use the blank canvas provided to record your musings and contemplations, and that this book will bring you encouragement, comfort and peace.

Week 1: Character

Coffee With Jesus: The Second Cup

"Jesus Christ, the Son of God, is the light that has defeated the darkness." - Excerpt, Day 4

Week 1: Character

Day One: Are You Recognizable?

Scripture: 1 John 4

Most of the Forward Operating Bases in Afghanistan are "blackout FOBs." That is, at night there are no lights. Doors and windows are covered up so that no interior lighting shines out. The only light available is from the moon. If it was cloudy, I relied on my trusty red penlight.

One evening as I was walking across a FOB I was visiting, I heard a voice call out, "CAPTAIN!" It has been a little while since I have been called that, but turned anyway, more out of instinct than anything else.

It turned out the voice belonged to a staff sergeant (SSG) I had worked with in the past who had recognized me as I was passing by. We chatted a bit, caught up on old times and I went on my way. A few days later, I bumped into the same SSG and he told me that he recognized me by my walk.

Apparently, I have a very distinct walk.

I still walk like a sailor – at sea – only on land. I have been told by a few people that I am recognizable simply by the way I carry myself.

As Christians, we ought to be recognized by the way we carry ourselves. There is a song I know called, "They'll Know We Are Christians By Our Love." I do not recall the originator, but it was the first song I learned to play on the guitar. It states in part:

And they'll know we are Christians/By our love, By our love/Yes, they'll know we are Christians By our love

We are one in Christ. And we are to be recognized by our love for one another. As Christians, that is how we should carry ourselves. If someone saw you in passing, would you be recognized based on how you carry yourself?

Coffee With Jesus: The Second Cup

Day Two: Good Fizbar!

Scripture: 2 Timothy 3:16-17

You're probably wondering, what in the world is "fizbar?" Fizbar, quite simply, is a made-up word. It means whatever time of day it is where you are. My boys and I made it up during one of our video chat sessions while I was deployed. Because of the time difference, evening in Afghanistan was morning where they lived and morning in Afghanistan was evening for them. It would get confusing saying good night or good morning, so we came up with the word "fizbar."

I have worked with people from many different nations, and I have realized that understanding is integral when it comes to communication. In fact, it is the essence of communication. For example, there was an Egyptian Army commander not too long ago who was convinced I spoke Arabic.

I do not speak Arabic.

I can say hello and goodbye in Arabic, but that's it. However, I knew what the Egyptian commander was talking about based on the context of our conversation. Based on the intent of the conversation I could answer his questions without the need for a translation. Context is very important when it comes to understanding when communicating.

Communicating with our Father is no different. His Word is essentially His conversation with us, but without context, the meaning can get lost or confused. When communicating with our Father, when having a conversation with Him through prayer and through study of His Word, it is very important that we pay attention to the context of what is being said.

Just as I do not speak Arabic but could understand the Egyptian commander by paying attention to context, we can understand God's Word by paying attention to context. I developed a relationship with the Egyptian commander through understanding. We can develop our relationship with the Lord the same way. It just takes listening, paying attention and knowing the context of the conversation.

Good Fizbar!

Week 1: Character

Day Three: God's Sabbath Rest

Scriptures: Matthew 11:28-30, Mark 2:23-28

My second tour in Afghanistan involved a lot of travel. I typically scheduled my trips so that I had a day or two between them. This helped me get caught up on paperwork and allowed me to refresh my travel bag.

When I was travelling with a coworker, whose area of responsibility was added to my own, I scheduled multiple trips back-to-back. This resulted in a lot of work with very little down time.

This marathon of travel always ended with a short trip to his neck of the woods before returning to my own "home away from home." Needless to say, after what was usually up to three weeks of non-stop travel, I was exhausted!

Life can get that way sometimes. It can get very busy, even overwhelming. Once, when Jewish leaders were questioning Jesus one time about actions His disciples were taking on the Sabbath, Jesus replied, "The Sabbath was made for man, not man for the Sabbath." (Mark 2:27). He went on to say that He was "Lord of the Sabbath. (v. 28)

When God rested on the 7th day, He did not do so for His own sake, but for ours. He knew that we would need to take time to recover from our work. While we are no longer under the law of Moses, it is still very important to take time to rest.

When life seems overwhelming, we can take solace in the fact that we can bring our burdens to Christ. We are creatures of body <u>and</u> soul. Take time in prayer to rest your spirit and also be sure to get your physical rest as well!

Coffee With Jesus: The Second Cup

Day Four: A Light in the Darkness

Scriptures: John 8:12, 2 Corinthians 4:5-6

One morning, I was sitting on my back porch. It was early, the gray before dawn. As I was sitting out there, listening to the wildlife wake up, I watched the sun slowly climb above the horizon. Eventually, it climbed over the trees and became visible.

It was bright! An intense, shining orb that I could not look at directly. While I could not see it directly, I could see its effects. The gray of the morning faded away, replaced by vivid, vibrant color. The light had pushed away the darkness, revealing the splendor of God's creation.

Sometimes, it seems as if we live in darkness. Sometimes, everything appears gray and dismal. It can be hard to find our way, and it can be hard to fathom the gray ever ending.

While it may seem the darkness cannot be beaten, we have a light that can overcome anything. The apostle John begins his Gospel by telling us, "In him was life, and that life was the light of all mankind. The light shines in the darkness, and the darkness has not overcome it." (John 1:4-5)

Jesus Christ, the Son of God, is the light that has defeated the darkness. He can help you overcome any darkness you are facing. "Cast all your anxiety on him because he cares for you." (1 Peter 5:7).

When you bring your worries and problems to Jesus, you will see the light penetrate and overcome the darkness. You will see the vivid, vibrant colors of life. Jesus can help you overcome any problem you are facing. Nothing is too small or too big for Him to handle.

Bring your problems to Jesus. Let His light shine through the darkness and you will see the dull gray of the dawn give way to the bright and vibrant with the colors of peace and comfort.

Week 1: Character

Day Five: It Starts with Us

Scriptures: Ephesians 4:2-3; 1 Corinthians 15:33

Have you ever wondered about how the world seems to be so filled with hate and anger? Division and strife? It can be overwhelming and anxiety inducing. In some ways, it seems like hate is becoming worse in our society. In other societies, it seems to be getting better. It felt like a strange dichotomy until I realized there are real and practical steps we can take to lower the amount of hate and strife in the world.

First, I changed how I interact with others, both in person and online. For a time, it seemed like I was losing both compassion for, and patience with, other people. I've been working to be both more compassionate and more patient with others. Granted, the results are mixed, but I can honestly say I am better now than I was a few years ago, although I'm still a work in progress.

Second, I changed who I interact with. Toxic people can have a severely negative impact on how you interact with others, and even who you are as a person. I found I was turning into someone I'm not. It was then that I decided to simply stop appeasing toxic people. That caused some friction and many of the toxic people showed themselves to the door. Some hung on and tried to get me to go back to appeasement, but finally I had to show them the door myself. The phrase "toxic people" may seem overused, but toxic people do exist and they can drag you down.

Eliminating hate begins with each of us. Two things you can do are 1) change how you interact with others, showing more compassion and patience (Ephesians 4:2-3), and 2) and change who you interact with. Toxic people can, and will, have an adverse effect on who you are and your well-being (1 Corinthians 15:33). It will be a work in progress, but you'll always be progressing and becoming a better person, closer to the person Jesus Christ knows you can be.

Coffee With Jesus: The Second Cup

Day Six: No Limits

Scripture: Job 36:22-24, Matthew 19:26, Luke 1:37

Have you ever tried to limit what you ask from God in your prayers? Have you ever started to ask for something, but then thought, "No, that's too much or not possible, I'll ask for this lesser thing, which is more possible instead."?

I once had a job that entailed a long walk from the parking lot to the building I worked in. One day, it was very stormy right at the time I was supposed to leave work. Knowing I had a long walk and seeing the dark clouds in the sky, I feared getting drenched before getting to my car. I was about to pray for God to hold off the rain and keep me dry when I thought to myself, "No, that's impossible, it's about to rain no matter what I'll pray that it's only light rain and that I don't get too wet, instead."

Just as I was about to make my silent request, I felt that still small voice ask me, "Do you think God can't do that? After all He's done for you, do you think he can't keep you dry?" I felt a little bad about my lack of faith and I realized that God had done some really huge things for me during my life. Surely keeping me dry would be nothing for Him. So, I told God I would be bold and I asked him to keep the rain at bay and keep me dry. Sure enough, the rain paused right around the time I had to leave my office and make the trek to my car. As I neared my car, it started to sprinkle a little, but it wasn't until I was in the car and driving home that the rain started in earnest. And yes, yours truly remained dry.

I realize some of you may be reading this and thinking to yourself, "Why would he ask to stay dry when there are so many horrible things happening in our world right now?" While you could argue the request was a silly one, the point is not the request itself, but the fact that God honored the request and answered it, without limits. I tried to impose my own limits on God, based on what I thought was possible, but with God, "All things are possible." Whether you want to stay dry on the way to your car, or seek healing for a loved one, don't limit God. Be bold, ask for what you want, and God will prove his power, without limit, if He chooses to do so.

Week 1: Character

Day Seven: Reeling in Serenity

Scripture: Mark 1:17

Fishing often has little to do with feeding our bodies. Rather, fishing most often feeds the soul.

In the stillness of the morning, we cast our lines into the glassy lake, watching as ripples fan out from the point of contact with the water. The sun rises, illuminating the landscape with a warm glow, and we bask in the tranquility of God's creation.

As the gentle waves lap against the boat, we remember that we can find solace in our own quiet moments with the Lord.

In Mark 1:17, Jesus calls out to Simon and Andrew, saying, "Come, follow me, and I will make you fishers of men." As we cast our lines and patiently wait for a bite, let us also remember to extend God's love and kindness to others, drawing them closer to Him as we navigate our lives together.

As the day unfolds and we reflect on the fish we have caught...or the ones that got away, we give thanks for the many blessings in our lives. Fishing reminds us of the value of patience, focus, and persistence—qualities that we can carry with us in our walk with Christ.

May we find moments of peace and serenity as we seek to follow in His footsteps, always casting our nets wide and reeling in hope and joy.

Coffee With Jesus: The Second Cup

Week 1 Notes

Week 1: Character

Coffee With Jesus: The Second Cup

Week 2: Reflections

Week 2: Reflections

Coffee With Jesus: The Second Cup

"As Christians, we will face storms of all types, but we worship One who is greater that all the storms of life combined."
- Excerpt, Day 3

Week 2: Reflections

Day One: Reflections on Lent

Scriptures: Matthew 4:1-11

The tradition of making a sacrifice for Lent, that is giving up some luxury or something you enjoy, goes back to when Jesus fasted in the desert for 40 days. Hence 40 days of sacrificing some luxury or pleasure. The purpose of this is to use that sacrifice to help you pray and to bring about change.

One year, I gave up swearing...well, I tried to give up swearing. The results...maybe not so good. BUT, by the end of that particular Lenten Season I was swearing much less and carried that change forward with me. In other years, I tried giving up things like Facebook. In the past, it was not too difficult, and I have always enjoyed the boost to my mental health that resulted from the much-needed break. In fact, I have taken breaks from social media outside of Lent as well. This particular year, however, it was more difficult than it had been in the past.

Of course, there was a major difference from past years; my family and I went through a major life transition during Lent, as I had just accepted an unaccompanied overseas job. Facebook is a very easy way to keep friends and family updated. Email works but making one single post on Facebook is so much easier than sending dozens of emails. With social media, people can get updates at their leisure, and I can keep emails relevant to the topics at hand. I'm not so conceited as to think people want to hear what I have to say, but I know that friends and family do like to stay updated.

So, this particular year, with the major transition, it was a struggle to keep people updated, which made this year's fast a true sacrifice. Isn't that the point though? It's supposed to be a sacrifice; one intended to help our prayer life and bring us closer to God. Lenten fasts are not supposed to be easy. They're some rote exercise that our church has us do each year. It is supposed to draw us nearer to God and help us meditate on Christ's sacrifice for us. I think, overall, it was worth it. How about you? What do you give up for Lent? Is the sacrifice worth it?

Coffee With Jesus: The Second Cup

Day Two: Reflections on Growth

Scripture: Hebrews 5:13-14; Hebrews 10:24-25

When I arrived in Qatar and moved into my new place, I had a new neighbor who was already living here. Soon after I moved in, my new friend hatched babies.

I watched them grow up, chirp when they were hungry, shiver when they were cold. I watch mom feed them and warm them. Then one day, just like that, they were gone! I went to make my coffee and noticed mom was once again by herself.

The babies grew up so fast.

It's symbolic in a way. As new Christians, we are like babies in Christ Jesus. Then we grow and mature, becoming full-fledged birds in our own right. The difference is, we never need to leave the nest. In fact, it is important to carry on in fellowship with other Christians.

Paul tells us two, equally important things about our Christian walks: 1) we should move on from spiritual milk to spiritual meat and 2) we should never give up meeting together. I believe these two things are linked. It is through Christian fellowship that we grow and mature, no longer being babes in Christ, but mature Christians who can help other babes in Christ grow and mature in their own right. As you become a spiritual parent, you will see your babies grow up so fast and become mentors in fellowship.

Week 2: Reflections

Day Three: Reflections on Rain

Scriptures: Matthew 8:23-27, Psalm 34:17-20, Nahum 1:7

The day started off normal enough, but when I opened the curtains, instead of the view of the Qatari neighborhood I was living in at the time, I noticed it was still dark. That was odd, it was the time of year when the sun rises earlier every day, not later. I thought it was weird, but I continued getting ready for my day.

Then, when I stepped outside to meet my ride, I noticed that the air was different. If felt different. It smelled different. It smelled like…rain. Then I felt it. It was subtle at first, fleeting, really. I wasn't quite sure if it happened or if it was my imagination. Then it happened a second time…then a third time. Yes, raindrops were hitting my arm. As my ride pulled up and I got in the car, the heavens opened! It was the first time since I had been here that it rained.

Rain can be exciting, but also scary. When storms blow through, they can wreak havoc. Ironically, as I am writing today's devotion, lightening is flashing, thunder is rolling and rain is pouring down outside. Storms can absolutely be scary! However, they are also necessary. After the storms have passed and the sun shines through, rain brings new life.

Spiritual storms are the same way. They can be scary and they can make you uncomfortable, but they can also bring new life. As Christians, we will face storms of all types, but we worship One who is greater that all the storms of life combined. You will get wet, you may even get soaked, but God will carry you through.

Are you going through a storm right now? Just hang on a little longer, God will calm your storms, dry you off and bless you even better than before.

Coffee With Jesus: The Second Cup

Day Four: Reflections on Scars

Scriptures: Psalm 147:1-3, Isaiah 40:28-31; 2 Cor 1:3-4

In Japan, when a piece of pottery breaks and then gets repaired, rather than try to hide the crack, they will fill that crack with gold. This is called Kintsugi. When the Japanese mend broken objects, they aggrandize the damage. They believe that when something becomes damaged, it has a history and becomes even more beautiful. This beauty is glorified by filling the cracks with gold.

Some years ago, I had surgery to remove a malignant melanoma. Right after that surgery, I had this big, angry, red scar on my neck. To be honest, it was a little embarrassing. There was no hiding it, no pretending it wasn't there. Eventually, I accepted the scar. I stopped trying to hide it. That scar indicated the removal of a deadly disease and spoke to my survival. That scar became a part of my personal history, a part of who I am.

As I've gone through life, I have increased my collection of scars and I've realized that they are nothing to be ashamed of. Each of us has our own scars. Some of them are physical and some are emotional. Whether they are physical or emotional, our scars are nothing to be ashamed of.

The Lord is bigger than anything that gives us scars. God provides for us: He provides healing, strength, comfort and restoration. It can be difficult to see this when we are weathering storms, but even in midst of the fiercest wind and rain, God is with us. He will carry us through and help us survive the storm. We may wind up scared by the experience, but that is OK. Those scars mean that you survived.

With God's strength, God's comfort and God's healing, you will overcome any storm that life will throw at you. So, let's not hide our scars, let's celebrate them. Take great pride in those scars! Those scars show that survived, that you have overcome and that you will overcome.

Week 2: Reflections

Day Five: Reflections on Worship

Scriptures: Isaiah 25:1; Exodus; Psalm 100:1-2; Acts 16:25

There is an old Rich Mullins song called "Above All." It's been covered by various Christian artists, including Rebecca St. James and Michael W. Smith. One morning while I was on my way to work, the Michael W. Smith version of the song came on the radio.

There was something about that song or the timing, and in that particular instance, as I sung the lyrics alone in my car, I could feel God's presence. Later that day, the song was playing in my head, and I felt a chill go down my spine. Once again, I felt God's presence, right there in my office.

When I was in Qatar I did not have a congregation to worship with, but I did find a way to hook my laptop up to the TV in my apartment and worship alone in my own way. I would then go to a popular video streaming site, find a playlist of some worship songs by my favorite artists and play the videos on my TV. Alone in my apartment, I was worshiping God. When I returned to the States, I found myself in my car, worshipping God alone again.

Fellowship and worship with your brothers and sisters is important, which is why the Bible tells us to do so (Hebrews 10:24-25). However, worship is not limited to being part of a group or at a specific time. God is with you wherever you are, so you can worship wherever you are: In your home, at your office, or driving your car. Location doesn't matter; your heart does.

Another popular Christian Contemporary song is "The Heart of Worship." So long as you have a worshipful heart, you can worship anytime, anywhere, so sing out as loud as you want.

Coffee With Jesus: The Second Cup

Day Six: Reflections On Revenge

Scripture: Matthew 5:43-48

I love the movie "The Princess Bride." I think it's a classic. When watching it with my boys, a lesser-known line jumped out at me as rather profound. In the scene where Inigo Montoya is explaining his background, he notes, "I just work for Vizzini to pay the bills. There's not a lot of money in revenge." He devoted his life to getting vengeance, but it was not a profitable endeavor.

Revenge is never profitable.

There have been people in my life that I have wanted to get revenge on. One such person was an unscrupulous landlord who threw my family out on the street while I was deployed to a warzone with the Army. I plotted, I planned, I even enjoyed it. But it wasn't profitable. As a matter of fact, I suffered for it. I became very angry and bitter. My prayer life suffered. I grew distant from God. I cried out, "God, help me forgive!"

God told me to pray for him. To pray that He would bless him. Wait, what?? " But God, you said that you would pay them back and you want me to pray for you to bless them?" Still, slowly...very, very slowly, I began to ask God to bless the very person I wanted to destroy. Somewhere along the way, something weird happened. I no longer wanted to destroy him.

The anger and bitterness were gone.

Eventually, after a LONG time of praying this prayer, I actually did mean it. I no longer had the thirst for vengeance that I once did. I was no longer plotting his demise and as a result, I was able to pray and read my Bible, eventually getting back to where I was in my walk with God. Forgiveness is not easy. It is the exact opposite of how we are inclined to treat those who wrong us. It takes a lot of time and effort, but it is every bit worth it.

There's not a lot of money in revenge...but there is great treasure in forgiveness.

Week 2: Reflections

Day Seven: Reflections on Holidays

Scriptures: Romans 14:4-9

It seems that every year, we have the same debates over the same holidays. Easter, Halloween, Christmas, each of them discussed at length. I am a little surprised Arbor Day is not included in the list.

Ok, maybe not, but why the debate? Why all the arguing? People will argue about customs, origins, theologies, legends, histories, you name it. The truth is, if you go digging deep enough, with a mind open enough, even the most sacred Christian holidays contain traditions with pagan origins.

Does it matter, though?

The birth, as well as the death, burial and resurrection, of Jesus are some of the most influential events in human history. I am firmly convinced that they need to be remembered and celebrated. Yes, over the centuries these holidays have taken on traditions that may not be Christian in origin, but does that matter?

In my own humble opinion what matters is who we are celebrating: Jesus Christ, our Lord, our Savior.

Paul tells us in Romans 14 that it's OK to celebrate holidays, and it's OK to not celebrate holidays. Romans 14 is a great chapter overall, as it talks about accepting each other as brothers and sisters in Christ, despite our differences. I think this chapter should apply to our attitudes about holidays as well.

It doesn't matter what holiday is in question. It doesn't matter what tradition is in question, just be fully convinced in your own mind and show some grace to your brothers and sisters in Christ.

What holidays do you like to celebrate? What are your favorite parts of those holidays? Celebrate. Enjoy. Share joy. Show love. Exhibit grace.

Week 2 Notes

Week 2: Reflections

Coffee With Jesus: The Second Cup

Week 3: Comfort

Week 3: Comfort

Coffee With Jesus: The Second Cup

"Have a request? Bring it before God. Need help? Ask it from God. No matter where you are, HE is with you." - Excerpt, Day 2

Week 3: Comfort

Day One: Help You Find Your Way

Scriptures: Psalm 32:8; 37:23-24; John 14:6

Soon after moving to a new city, I had some errands to run. Being new to town, I only knew one particular area and the errands were in an area that I was unfamiliar with. I tried using a map app, but things didn't go quite as I planned and I soon found myself very lost.

I saw a Chic-Fil-A restaurant and pulled into the drive-through to get some lunch. While waiting for my food, I checked the map app again and I could not make heads or tails of where I was or how to get back to where I needed to be. I was well and truly lost.

Eventually, by complete chance and with no clear idea of where I was, I managed to find my way to a hardware store that was my last errand for the day. Not only that, it turned out the hardware store was on the way home. While walking into the store, I said a prayer of thanks. There is no doubt in my mind that God helped me find my way. As I was walking the aisles of the store, I realized that God has helped me find my way often.

God has helped me find my way not just literally, like when I was lost that day trying to do errands, but also when I was lost in a deeper sense of the word. Lost in sin? God helped me find my way out. Lost emotionally? God helped me find my way out. Lost Spiritually? Hopefully you've caught onto a pattern now... God helped me find my way out.

Everyone gets lost sometimes. You may have been lost recently, or you may be lost now. Physically, emotionally, spiritually, everyone can be lost in different ways and at different times. If you find yourself lost, whether it is lost in sin, lost emotionally, lost physically or lost spiritually, you can always turn to God.

He will help you find your way. I know he will because has He helped me and continues to do so whenever I need a guiding light.

Day Two: God is With Us

Scripture: Jeremiah 23:24; Philippians 4:6-7; Psalm 139:7-12;

During one period of my life, I was not a regular attending member of any specific church or congregation. I was in a new area, still getting settled, and had not yet found the opportunity for fellowship with my brothers and sisters in Christ. I still set aside my own personal quiet time, but that corporate worship was lacking. As a result, it felt like worship in general was lacking as well. There is a lot to be said for fellowship and worship within the body of Christ. However, I realized it was also possible to worship God no matter where you are. Worship is not about a place or who you are with. Worship is about WHO you are worshiping.

God is with us, no matter where we are. This doesn't just apply to worship, either. Have a request? Bring it before God. Need help? Ask it from God. No matter where you are, HE is with you. He hears your prayers whether you are at church or at work, in your home and in your car. Everywhere.

Omnipresence is one of God's greatest traits, because He can help us, comfort us or grant us strength no matter where we are. I mentioned in an earlier devotion how fellowship with our brothers and sisters is important. And it is! However, God is not limited to a particular building that is used for meeting up with our brothers and sisters in Christ. God is not limited to any location, anywhere.

No matter what you are struggling with, and no matter where you are, you can bring your requests to God. He will hear you and He will help you because no matter where you are, God is right beside you, waiting to give you the support, comfort and help you need.

Week 3: Comfort

Day Three: God is in the Details

Scriptures: Isaiah 41:10; Philippians 4:6-7; John 14:1

When I was leaving the navy, I was due to fly to Houston from Japan. I decided I would try a little experiment. Previously, I would fret every little detail, praying for help as every little problem arose. While there is nothing wrong with praying for help, I did so more out of anxiety then I did out of faith. This time, I told God that I would trust Him to be in control. If any problems came up during the trip, I would not fret or get anxious, I would simply trust in Him. Not only did things not go wrong, things went more smoothly than I ever could have imagined.

As I was getting ready to leave for another deployment to Afghanistan, this time as a government civilian, I once again looked at all the things that could go wrong. I decided, before leaving home, that I would take the same approach as I did in Japan. I asked God to be in control again. Not just with the flight, but for the entire week of training. The only direction I had received from the base here was to go to the USO and ask about the shuttle, but God was in Control, so I got on the plane, they closed the doors and I was on my way.

Sure enough, just like the trip back from Japan, God was not only in the details, but He exceeded my expectations. I left home, made it through training and made it overseas without any issues. Things again went more smoothly than I could have imagined.

I have learned since then that while life will not always go smoothly, I do not need to worry about every little thing, as I am prone to do. Instead, I can bring the entire situation to God and let him handle it. I know from experience that is easier said than done. However, I also know from experience that when I do, God not only takes care of things, he does so in a way that exceed my expectations. Are you in a stressful situation? Bring it to God. Let him handle it. God will take of things. God is in the details.

Coffee With Jesus: The Second Cup

Day Four: It's OK to Fail

Scripture: Judges 16:25-30; Isaiah 19:11-14

I am a failure.

It's true. I am a failure.

I tried starting my own business, not once, but twice. Failed both times. I tried taking the Professional Engineer license exam and failed it. Not once, but twice. I failed to get promoted in both the navy AND the army...again, not once, but twice.

I published four books, three of which were total failures.
But the fourth one? It's a steady seller. It's not NYT Bestseller material, but it is a steady performer.

And you know what? I'm going to publish a fifth book. I'm going to take the PE exam a third time. I may even try starting my own business again. Why? Why would I do that after failing so many times?

Because failing doesn't matter. Failing more than once doesn't matter. It's not about how many times you fail, but how many times you try.

If you don't try, you won't succeed. If you fail and don't try again, you won't succeed. But if you fail and fail again, and fail yet again, and keep trying, eventually you will succeed.

Some of the greatest Bible characters were failures: King David slept with a married woman and murdered her husband. Sampson was a hero of Israel and was betrayed by his lover after he told her the secret of his strength (his hair). God restored both after their failures and God will help you through yours as well.

Never stop trying. Fail once, fail twice, fail fifty times. Never stop trying. On one of those tries, you WILL succeed.

Week 3: Comfort

Day Five: Driving Through Rainbows

Scriptures: Genesis 9:13-16; Joshua 1:5,9; John 10:29

One weekend while I was out driving with my oldest boy running some errands, we got caught in a sun shower. Well, I say, "shower" but it was raining buckets. It was coming down hard, but the sun was still shining. This combination produced a rainbow. At first, it was just over the trees, but soon, it was on the road. Then it appeared right in front of us, and we drove right through it.

The rainbow is a symbol of God's promise. Noah beheld a rainbow after he survived the flood and knew it for what it was, a sign of God's promise. . God promised that He would never again destroy all life on Earth by a flood. This was an everlasting promise made by God to all people. Today, God promises us so much more, and the rainbow has come to mean so much more. To some, the rainbow is a sign of all God's promises.

One of God's biggest promises is that He will never leave us. God is with us in our times of plenty, and He is with us in our time of need. No matter what you may be going through, no matter what storm you are weathering, God is with you. No storm, circumstance or need can overcome God's love for you or separate you from His awesome power.

Sometimes, while in the midst of a storm, it can be tough to feel God's presence. We have trouble seeing Him and may think He is not there. When my daughter was little, she liked to play hide and seek. She would cover her head with the blanket to "hide." She reasoned that if she couldn't see me, I wasn't there, even when I was sitting right next to her.

Just like I was right next to my daughter when she couldn't see me, God is next to us, even when we can't see or feel him. He promises to always be with us. He is there with you through your darkest storm. We can know He is with us because has promised to never leave us. And we are reminded that the Lord keeps His promises every time we see a rainbow.

Day Six: Fly Away Free

Scriptures: 2 Corinthians 1:3-5

Did you ever have one of those "God moments?" You know the kind; the type of things that are too much to be a mere coincidences? I've had many such moments, but one in particular stands out. I was recording an episode of my podcast, "Coffee With Jesus," and had a guest for that particular episode.

While we were talking, she stopped suddenly and with a slight chuckle said, "This is not what I had planned to talk about." Immediately preceding that, she had said that sometimes God can use our struggles and the comfort that we receive from Him, to provide comfort to others. The reason I consider this a "God moment" is because while recording an earlier episode a few days prior I had said the same thing myself. I was editing that very episode earlier on the day that I had interviewed this guest.

Two episodes, two separate individuals, one message. The same message:

Sometimes God comforts us so that we can spread that same comfort to others.

Spreading comfort, hope and encouragement is the main mission of "Coffee With Jesus". It is the purpose of the podcast and it is my hope that you will find comfort in the pages of this devotional, as well.

Yesterday, we saw that God will never leave us or forsake us. We saw that God will provide us with the comfort we need at the time that we will need it. Let's take the comfort that we have received and pass it on to others. When you are going through life's storms, God will provide you with the hope, comfort and encouragement you need. When your storm has passed, you can help provide that same hope, comfort and encouragement to others.

Week 3: Comfort

Day Seven: Have You Ever Danced with God?

Scripture: Hebrews 13:5

There are too many storms these days. I don't know what you're going through—the aftermath of a physical storm or maybe something internal, but I do know this: God loves you more than you can imagine. And even if you can't see Him, He is right there with you. I learned this on one of the scariest nights of my life.

Through the porthole of a sailboat I was crewing on, I could see the captain dangling from the mast out over the dark sea. I shook my head. "We're never going to live through this!" Bone-weary, I crawled into bed. With the boat at a ninety-degree angle, I planted my feet against the foot of the bed and braced myself against the wall, holding tightly to the bunk above so I wouldn't fall into the sloshing water below. I pulled my lips over my teeth and bit hard when that threatening voice inside my head took up a chant, "We're gonna' die. We're gonna' die." The boat rose, pitched, and then fell as the bottom dropped out from underneath us. And just when I thought we were going down, we crashed, and I crumbled. The boat can't handle this. It's going to fall apart. "God," I whimpered, "If You save me, I'll do whatever You want!"

As if I had hit a switch, a presence filled the room. With my eyes open, as if dreaming, but awake, I saw Jesus. Not like I could see my friend lying in the bunk above. Not in physical form, but ethereal. I gulped, as understanding flooded me. "You've been here. I tried to get away, but You've been here the whole time!" And there I'd stood, as if I'd had my hand on His chest, pushing Him away. Seeing Him now, I realized we'd been stuck in this pose for a long time. I hadn't wanted Him to go in case I needed Him, but I hadn't wanted Him to boss me around, either. Ever so patiently— suspended in time, but oh-so-very present—Jesus held out His hand and invited me to dance. "Yes," I yielded, and something so much more peaceful than peace settled inside even though the circumstances hadn't budged. "Let's dance."

Whatever it is you're going through, it's not too much for God. He may just want you to let go and let Him handle it while you dance.

Coffee With Jesus: The Second Cup

Week 3 Notes

Week 3: Comfort

Coffee With Jesus: The Second Cup

Week 4: God Is…

Week 4: God Is…

Coffee With Jesus: The Second Cup

"God can protect us from little things and from big things. No matter what size storm you are facing, God can protect you."
- Excerpt, Day 2

Week 4: God Is...

Day One: Our Refuge

Scriptures: Psalm 91:1-4

One evening in Afghanistan while I was sitting in my room after a long day the sirens went off. I dutifully went to the bunker and soon we were given the signal for "All clear", meaning the rockets had stopped and I could return to my room. However, 15 minutes later the sirens went off again. More rockets and mortars landing around us.

This went on for literally hours. We would come under attack, then get the "All Clear", then get attacked again, then get the "All Clear". After a few repetitions of this, we decided to just stay in the bunker. The bunker was our place of safety, our refuge from the rockets and mortars.

At one point, I turned to a buddy in frustration and said, "They need to knock this off. I need my beauty sleep!"

My buddy looked at me and replied, "Yeah and you need all the beauty sleep you can get!"

It was a light moment in a dark hour. Eventually, the dark hour came to an end. The bunker, our refuge, had protected us and kept us safe.

When life sends rockets and mortars your way, God is your bunker. He is your sanctuary in your time of trouble. You can take refuge in Him. He will take care of you and give you peace.

Bring all your troubles to God. Take refuge in Him and you too will be able to get your beauty sleep.

Coffee With Jesus: The Second Cup

Day Two: Our Protector

Scriptures: Psalm 91:5-8

During my second tour in Afghanistan, I went to a base in the southern part of the country that was considered "safe." It was a small Forward Operating Base (FOB) that had not been attacked in over a year. Well, my luck was such that the morning I arrived that FOB was attacked. I was sitting in my quarters just after breakfast, when I heard and felt an explosion so big that it knocked the heater right off my wall (the wall of one of the CHUs in that row was actually blown in).

It was so loud and so intense that my first thought was a mortar had landed right outside. My second thought being, "if that was the case, why am I not dead?" It turned out that a mortar round had not impacted right next to me. What had actually happened was approximately 1500 pounds, three quarters of a ton of High Explosives was detonated right outside the wall of the FOB. The explosion happened about 400 meters away (that's about 1.5 American football fields, give or take). The concussion wave from explosion caused damage to buildings a full kilometer away.

This just one of many explosions I lived through during my time in Afghanistan. I know what it's like to take shelter from rockets and mortars and I know what it's like to actually feel explosions that are nearby. I know the stress and anxiety that go along with it.

I also know firsthand the protection God provides. Not only did He keep me safe that day, He kept every soldier on the base safe. God can protect us from little things and from big things. No matter the ferocity of the storm you find yourself in, God can protect you. Bring your concerns to Him today and let His protection carry you through.

Week 4: God Is…

Day Three: Our Strength

Scriptures: Psalm 46:1; Psalm 73:26

God is our strength and our shield. He is our refuge and our fortress. God does not promise to keep every storm away, but He does promise to be with us in every storm we face. He is our strength and will help us persevere no matter what trial we are enduring.

Both when I was in the Navy and also later on while I was the Army (after my Navy career), I had to run twice a year as part of a semi-annual physical fitness test. Running is my least favorite activity. I've never been an able runner and even when I was in peak shape, running was difficult for me. To add to my difficulty, when I was in the Army, I had to do this physical test at an altitude of over 6,000 feet!

Running was tough for me at the best of times, and now at over a mile in altitude where oxygen is much scarcer than at sea level, I had to run two miles. To be honest with you, it was a struggle, but I pushed on and I made it to the finish line. Paul tells us that he, "press[es] on toward the goal for the prize of the upward call of God in Christ Jesus." (Philippians 3:14, ESV).

Sometimes it feels like we don't have the strength to run the race. I know I certainly felt that way when taking my physical test in Afghanistan. Spiritually, it can also be that way! Often we feel that we lack the spiritual strength to keep moving.

In those cases, God will be your strength. God will provide you with what you need to keep going.

Turn all of your struggles over to God. When you don't have the strength to continue, whether it's physical, emotion, spiritual or any other combination, take things to God and let HIM be your strength.

Coffee With Jesus: The Second Cup

Day Four: Our Deliverer

Scriptures: Psalm 91:1-3

During my first tour in Afghanistan, I was once part of a team that went to a local village to meet up with the village elders and a local contractor who was building a well and pumphouse to provide water to the village. As was typical on these missions, we met up with the local Afghan police. The police would be our escort for the day.

We brought four, twenty-gallon cans filled with gasoline. We loaded up, left the base and met our escorts. Eventually they led us to what can best be described as a town square.

Then they vanished.

Such a thing was not uncommon in Afghanistan. The local police would sometimes lead coalition forces into ambushes after being paid by the Taliban.

In our case, we all braced for what we knew was coming. The local police were gone for what seemed like hours. Where they had led us was a perfect spot for an ambush. We waited for the inevitable...

And then the police returned. Just like that. No ambush, no attack. The local police forces came back, guiding us to our destination.

In our after-action meeting, it was pretty well agreed that the plan had been to ambush us, but the general feeling was that the twenty gallons of gas that we had provided was enough to keep them from betraying us.

I have a different take. I think it was God who protected us that day. The Lord is our fortress. No matter what enemy we may be facing, in Him we can take refuge.

Week 4: God Is…

Day Five: Our Healer

Scriptures: Matthew 4:23; James 5:14

In the summer of 2023, after having successfully avoided it for three years, I came down with COVID. At first, I thought it was the flu. Those were the symptoms I had. Still, I took an at home test just to be sure. The results were negative.

A few days later, as my symptoms continued to worsen, I went to the doctor for a more sensitive test. This time, the results were positive: I had COVID. For me, it was like a really bad case of the flu, but then my throat and ears got infected.

I was in quite a bit of pain. It seemed like it would never end. I cried out to God, and our Father heard my prayers.

The fever went away, then the headaches, then the congestion. Finally, even the sore throat and earaches were gone.

The Bible recounts many healing miracles by the prophets, by Jesus and by the Apostles. Even when the prophets and Apostles appeared to heal others, it was by GOD's power that people were healed.

God can, and does, heal us today. Jesus is often referred to as "The Great Physician."

Are you sick? Bring it to God. Ask your brothers and sisters in Christ to pray for you. God can and does heal us, even today. I know He does, because He healed me.

Coffee With Jesus: The Second Cup

Day Six: Our Helper

Scriptures: Titus 2:7-8, 1 Peter 3:14-16

Last week, I shared the story of how God stayed the rain while I made the long trek from my office to my car. As I shared that story with some friends, an old navy buddy told me, "When people argue about the triviality of the request in a world that is so messed up, they too are imposing limits on God by assuming He can only do so many things at once, and that keeping you dry must have resulted in calamity somewhere else."

His response was very insightful, and it reinforced the fact that it is OK to ask God for help with the "little things." Lost your keys? Can't find your phone? Important task at work? Ask God for help. It is important to know that God is with us and will help us with what we perceive to be smaller things, as well as those things we perceive to be bigger in nature. Equally important, in my humble view, is taking the time to thank God for the little things as well.

One morning, soon after moving into a new home, my son and I went to a storage unit to get out some items we needed. We loaded up our vehicle at the storage unit and set out to return to our new home. We had gone just around the corner when the skies opened up. It was raining and raining hard. If we had waited just a few more minutes, we would have been caught in the rain as we were loading up the car. We would have been drenched, and our boxes would have become waterlogged, likely ruining whatever what was inside them.

However, we made it just in the nick of time. Both us and our boxes remained dry inside the car. I quickly realized that God was looking out for us. As I drove home through the rain, I said a small prayer of thanks. I had not anticipated the weather, but God had, and He took care of us. While this may seem like a small thing to some people, I think it's important to thank God for all things, even the small things that may seem insignificant.

Take the time to ask God for help in <u>all</u> things, and take time to give the Lord thanks, even for the little things.

Week 4: God Is...

Day Seven: Our Comforter

Scriptures: Matthew 11:28-29; Romans 8:26-28

One of the worse periods of my life in the aftermath of Hurricane Katrina. My family and I lost everything we owned. Every day seemed to bring a new fight. First it was a fight for our survival. No home, no job, no clothes except what we brought with us.

Then, although we realized that we would survive, we still had to fight with bill collectors, credit card companies, the mortgage company... even the insurance company! That's right, we had insurance that was supposed to cover our losses, but after the assessment, they wouldn't send us the money they owed us, and their story kept changing as to why.

It was a very difficult time overall, but one thing kept me going. One thing allowed me to keep my head up high: The comfort of our loving Father.

Sometimes we are so close to rock bottom we don't even know what form our prayers should take nor what to ask for. As I've mentioned often, sometimes all I could say was, "God, Help!" And that's OK. When we are unable to pray, when we don't even know what to say, the Holy Spirit will "...intercede for us with groanings too deep for words." (Romans 8:27)

God knows what we need before we even ask. While He loves it when we bring our cares and worries to Him (Matt 11:28), He knows that sometimes we are simply unable to give words to our worries.

That's OK, too. Our Father is not only our strength, He is our comfort. What do you need help with? Are you struggling to even find the words? Go to the Lord. He WILL comfort you, even if all you can say is "God, help!"

Coffee With Jesus: The Second Cup

Week 4 Notes

Week 4: God Is...

Coffee With Jesus: The Second Cup

Week 5: Recovery

Week 5: Recovery

Coffee With Jesus: The Second Cup

"God's Word holds answers to questions you didn't even know you had yet!" - Excerpt, Day 3

Week 5: Recovery

Day One: Give It to God

Scriptures: James 5:14-16

When I was a teenager… ohhhh… a few years ago… I was at a men's retreat at my church. It was a great spirit-filled weekend with some wonderful fellowship.

When the retreat had concluded and we were all preparing to go our separate ways, we discovered that one of our number was having some vehicle issues.

Of course, we all rushed over to help, myself in the lead. Our "help" mostly consisted of us giving him obvious instructions like "Pop the hood" and "Try turning her over again." As we stood around staring at the engine and trying to ascertain what the issue was, nothing seemed to work or help.

Eventually, someone asked us all, "Well, has anyone prayed about it yet?"

We all looked chagrined. We had all tried to fix thing our way, instead of bringing it to God first. After some embarrassed glances all around, we gathered around the engine and prayed together. Then, with one more "try turning it over again…"

The engine started right up! We prayed. God answered. The vehicle worked!

Is there something in your life that doesn't seem to be working? Have you tried fixing it yourself to no avail? Give it to God. Our Father will fix it for you.

Coffee With Jesus: The Second Cup

Day Two: Talk to God

Scriptures: Matthew 18:19; Mark 11:2

What is prayer?

Prayer, quite simply, is a conversation with our Heavenly Father. It can be a request for help, or it can be to praise Him for help He has already provided. I can be a way of seeking guidance on big decisions or simply an expression of gratitude, a "thank you", for no reason in particular. It can also be to thank Him for blessings we have received and for things that are going well in our lives but one does not need to pray with an "agenda"; it can simply be a way to connect with God in any way that you are comfortable with. It's a conversation between our Father and one of his children.

There is no set way to pray. There is no magic formula nor secret recipe. To pray you can simply talk to our Father in Heaven as you would talk to a close and dear friend. Jesus tells us, "Whatever you ask for in my name, will be granted by my Father."

Are you in need? Are you facing a major storm in your life? Are you in need of guidance? It doesn't matter how big or how small your problem may seem, nothing is too big or too small for the Creator of the Universe! The very idea of labeling our problems as "big" or "small" based on comparing to them to how we perceive others' problems, as if there is a scorekeeper keeping track of everyone's trials and tribulations and ranking them, gives short thrift to God's desire to help YOU with YOUR problems. Let Him.

Talk to God. Tell Him what you need. Ask Him to help you through life's storms. Our Father will help you. He will never let you down.

Prayer is powerful. Prayer is effective. Prayer works!

Week 5: Recovery

Day Three: Read God's Word

Scriptures: 2 Timothy 3:16-17; Hebrews 4:12

It's often said that prayer is how we talk to God, and the Bible is how God talks to us. The Bible is more than just a love letter, more than just an instruction manual, more than a list of "Do's" and "Do not's". The Bible is God's divinely inspired Word. It holds the answers to all your questions. God's Word holds answers to questions you didn't even know you had yet!

God's Word can help us overcome temptation (Matt 4:1-11), parry attacks from the enemy (Ephesians 6:17) and equip us for the work that the Lord has laid out for us to do (2 Timothy 3:17).

Prayer is powerful, and so is the Bible. There is a reason that the Bible is the single most read book in history. It is "alive and active, sharper than any double-edged sword" (Hebrews 4:12).

When we read God's Word, we are not just looking at words on a page. We are transforming ourselves. We are growing closer to our Father in Heaven. We are becoming more mature in our walk. God's Word is powerful. God's Word is authoritative. With it and through it we can become equipped to serve our Father in any task He calls us to.

Entire volumes, concordances and commentaries have been written on God's Word, but today, I would like to encourage you to take the time, if you don't already do so, to read it with no intermediary. You do not have to be a scholar to understand what it says. All you need is faith, willingness and a little bit of discipline to take the time and open yourself up to the wonders of the Bible.

My prayer for you today is that you will read God's Word and in doing so, grow closer to the author of the Word.

Coffee With Jesus: The Second Cup

Day Four: Listen to God

Scriptures: Psalm 119:105; John 1:1-3

God speaks to us in many ways. In the past, God has spoken to some through dreams and visions. To others, God speaks to them as a quiet, small voice. To most people, our Heavenly Father speaks to us through His Word.

Our relationship with the Lord is dependent on communication. Effective communication goes both ways. When we pray, we are talking to God, but when we listen, when we are receptive to what He has to say, we can take our spiritual walk to a whole new level.

God speaks to different people in different ways. Maybe God has spoken to you in a dream. Maybe God has spoken to you through His spirit, with that quiet, small voice. Maybe God spoke to you through His Word, with a particular scripture jumping off the page and having a lasting impact.

In yesterday's reading, we saw how important God's Word is. Today I would like to expand on that. The Bible, with words written thousands of years ago, can be our guide today. Sometimes, when you ask for God's direction, He will lead you to a passage that "pops," a passage whose words apply directly and exactly to what you are preoccupied with.

I firmly believe that God speaks to us by many different means. The key is for us to <u>listen</u>. By listening to God, we can discern His will. By listening to God, we can make the right decisions. By listening to God, we can follow the path that He has laid out for us.

Why not take some time today, find a quiet place and listen? See what God has to say to you. You will find your walk with Him is better than it ever was before.

Week 5: Recovery

Day Five: Perseverance

Scriptures: Romans 5:3-5; James 1:2-4

The year 2024 was very difficult for me. There was a lot of loss. My father passed, as did two of my college friends and one of my high school friends. There was financial loss as my son totaled my car, and as I had to support him during his co-op during the summer. The loss of my father took a financial toll, as well, with the unplanned trips to my parents' home both before and after he passed.

For a while, it seemed like the hits just kept coming. For some reason, I just could not catch a break! I felt like just as I survived one storm, another torrent just arriving.

Through all of it, I was able to keep going. Not by virtue of my own strength, not by a long shot, but with the strength of our Father in Heaven. The Lord was with me through each and every trial. He was holding me through each loss I faced.

Sometimes, we do not have the strength to continue, but through the Lord, we can use His strength to persevere. I will admit that I am weak. There was more than one occasion when I felt like I couldn't do it anymore, but God would not let me quit. God gave me the strength I needed to carry on.

God will give you that same strength. He is right there with you, at this very moment. Our Father has an infinite supply of strength to give you. All you need to do is ask.

With God's strength, you can endure any storm. With God's strength you can carry on no matter what life throws at you.

With God's strength, you can persevere.

Coffee With Jesus: The Second Cup

Day Six: Spread Hope

Scripture: Romans 7:14-25

Today I share with you a special message of hope..

The mission of Coffee With Jesus Ministries is to spread hope and comfort, especially when those things are hard to find. The goal of this book is to do the same, to spread comfort and hope.

Today's world can be scary. There are saber rattles of possible new wars daily, natural disasters, oil prices rise and fall, the stock market rises and falls and inflation seems like it will never end.

We are, indeed, living in some trying times. New variants of diseases are being discovered, and food is getting hard to find. The stress and anxiety you are feeling are normal.

I would like to tell you that in spite of all of this, everything is going to be OK.

Allow me to repeat myself: Everything is going to be ok.

Now say it to yourself.

God is in control during the good times and during the scary times. Look to our Father and he will provide you with peace, with comfort and with hope.

Everything is going to be OK.

Week 5: Recovery

Day Seven: Spread Comfort

Scriptures: Corinthians 14:1-4

When most people think of a prophet, they think of a seer or an oracle. Someone who can divinely predict or interpret the future. The Bible, however, tells us a different story. According to the Bible, a prophet is a messenger of God who brings comfort, strength and encouragement to the Body of Christ.

You don't need any special talents to do spread hope, just a willing heart. Many tend to get caught up in the word "prophet" or "prophecy" as a gift. If those words give you cause for pause, that's OK. Words tend to change over time, taking on new meanings or different connotations altogether.

The point is not necessarily what a prophet is or is not, but rather, our ability and willingness to bring comfort and encouragement to others:

> **When Elijah was battling depression, God didn't send an angel to preach to him, tell him to pray more, rebuke him or condemn him. He sent an angel to comfort him while he rested. Sometimes, a person just needs comfort.**

Sometimes, a person just needs comfort. That's what all of us should be doing, bringing comfort to our brothers and sisters. Instead of getting hung up on terminology and definitions, ask yourself, "How can I comfort someone else today?"

Week 5 Notes

Week 5: Recovery

Coffee With Jesus: The Second Cup

Week 6: Above and Beyond

Coffee With Jesus: The Second Cup

"As Christians, we have an eternal hope. This hope goes beyond grief, even beyond loss." - Excerpt, Day 2

Week 6: Above and Beyond

Day One: Beyond Hate

Scriptures: Ephesians 4:2-3; 1 Corinthians 15:33

Does it bother you as much as it bothers me how the world seems to be so filled with hate and anger? With division and strife? It can be overwhelming and anxiety inducing. In some ways, it seems like hate is becoming worse in our society. In other ways, it seems to be getting better. It feels like a strange dichotomy, but I've come to realize there are real and practical steps we can take to lower the amount of hate and strife in the world.

First, I've changed how I interact with others, both in person and online. For a while, it seemed like I was losing compassion for, and patience with, other people. To counteract this, I've been working to be both more compassionate and more patient with others. Granted, the results are mixed, but I can honestly say I am better now than I was two years ago, and I am still "a work in progress."

Second, I've changed who I interact with. Toxic people can have a severely negative impact on how you interact with everyone, even people who aren't toxic, and it can even change who you are as a person. I found I was turning into someone I didn't like. To reverse this, I decided to simply stop appeasing toxic people. That, unsurprisingly. caused some friction and many of the toxic people showed themselves the door and left my circle. Some hung on and tried to get me to continue to appease them, but finally I showed them the door, too. The phrase "toxic people" may seem like it is overused, but toxic people do exist and they can easily drag you down if you don't take steps to be true to yourself.

Eliminating hate begins with us. Two things you can do are: 1) change how you interact with others, showing more compassion and patience (Ephesians 4:2-3) and 2) change who you interact with. Toxic people can and will adversely affect who you are and your well-being (1 Corinthians 15:33). It will be a work in progress, but you'll always be working towards progress.

Coffee With Jesus: The Second Cup

Day Two: Beyond Death

Scriptures: Psalm 34:18; John 11:35, Revelation 21:4

The phone call came in the middle of the night; my father had passed away.

He had been fighting cancer for a while. The cancer had metastasized and spread all over his body. The treatments put him the hospital with congestive heart failure. At the time I received the news, my father had been back in the hospital for about a week. Somehow, I knew he would be going to his spiritual home instead of his terrestrial one.

There were regrets over what could have been. There was guilt over not having visited more recently. And there was the deep, deep sense of loss at not being able to have another conversation with my dad.

However, there was also some relief. My father had been severely suffering for some time. Now his suffering was over. He was in Heaven in his new, perfect body. In the midst of my grief, I took comfort in the knowledge that there is no sickness in Heaven.

As Christians, we have eternal hope. This hope goes beyond grief, even beyond loss. This hope gave me great comfort when I needed it most. Through Jesus Christ, we have eternal life with our Heavenly Father. Jesus told us, "My Father's house has many rooms; if that were not so, would I have told you that I am going there to prepare a place for you? And if I go and prepare a place for you, I will come back and take you to be with me that you also may be where I am." (John 14:2-3).

We have a room in a Heavenly mansion. While the grief of loss was heavy, it was tempered by the notion that I will see my dad again. He is living in his new perfect body, in a room that Jesus has prepared for him. Someday, I will be in my own room near my dad and we will have a lot of catching up to do!

Week 6: Above and Beyond

Day Three: Beyond Moving

Scriptures: Psalm 54:4; Psalm 121:1-2; Romans 8:26-27

We hadn't even fully settled into our new place when I received an email from the landlord: The owner wanted to sell his house and we would have to move in a few months.

Moving is hard. Moving is expensive. We had not yet recovered from our move and we were looking at the second move within a year. This meant looking for a new place, saving up for deposits and other moving costs, and girding ourselves for the intense labor that moving involved.

In fairness, we were renters, and the owner was free to sell if he wanted to. He would honor the lease we had signed, but we would not be able to sign another. I'll admit I panicked. I can honestly say that I immediately started praying, but if I am being even more honest, I didn't fully trust in God. I tried to plan everything and handle everything myself.

Then, one evening when I was at the end of my rope, I cried out to God, "God, if you can give us just a few more months in this place, I will go to church every week!" You can imagine my surprise when, a few days later, I received another email from the landlord: the owner is going to wait to sell, would we be interested in staying? We wound up signing a three-month lease, which gave us just the reprieve we needed.

With my father having just passed away and my youngest child about to graduate from college, this small reprieve was huge! But that's not all. A few weeks later, there was yet another email from the landlord: The owner was not going to sell, would we like to extend our lease out a full year? The answer was a very quick, "YES!"

I should have gone to God first, and I should have trusted in Him more. When we go to God, He not only will take care of us, He will go above and beyond. He will help us beyond what we can imagine. Are you going through a storm right now? Take it to God. Let him handle it. He will not only help you, but He will help you more than you can imagine!

Coffee With Jesus: The Second Cup

Day Four: The Cat Came Back

Scripture: 2 Thessalonians 3:16; Philippians 4:6-7

The day I received the news about my dad, I also learned of a big thunderstorm forecast to arrive the next day. I dutifully brought in various outside items that could be blown around and cause damage: chairs, flowerpots, bird feeders, etc.

I opened the garage to temporarily store all the things I had collected in preparation for the storm. Unfortunately, in the state of mind I was in, I forgot to close the garage. One of my cats, Maxine, a beautiful Maine Coone mix, decided to make a break for it and explore the outside world beyond the walls of our home. I didn't realize that she had left until it was time for her evening feeding. I put out her food, but she didn't show up. I looked for her in all her usual hiding spaces. She was nowhere to be found. During my search for her, I discovered my dreadful mistake: the garage door was still open.

I was devastated. I had just been hit with news of my father's death. Now my cat had run off and, to make matters worse, it was my fault. I had carelessly left the garage door open and she had taken the opportunity to explore the neighborhood, as any curious cat naturally would.

In this case, I can truthfully say that I went to God first. I begged him to bring my cat home. As soon as I prayed, I felt a sense of peace. The anxiety, fear and guilt all faded away. I knew, I can't explain how, that my cat would be home by breakfast. The next morning, before the sun even rose, I grabbed a container of her treats and went outside, shaking the container of treats as I went. I only got as far as one house down the street when she trotted up, oblivious to the angst she had caused, expecting her food.

The Bible tells us that when we bring our requests to God, "...the peace of God which transcends all understanding will guard your heart and your mind in Christ Jesus." (Phil 4:7). Are you anxious? Are you desperate? Are you experiencing a devastating storm? Bring it to God! He will give you peace... a peace that will guard your heart and your mind in Christ Jesus.

Week 6: Above and Beyond

Day Five: Beyond College 1

Scriptures: Psalm 139:13-14; Hebrews 4:16

My Father's passing, the pending move, the missing cat... they all happened at the same time. In addition, during this time as we were also preparing for my youngest child's college graduation.

Fortunately, by the time graduation came, the cat came back, and we were given a three-month extension on our lease. Both things were quite a blessing. Now, we could focus on the graduation and moving my kid out of the college dorm for the last time.

There was a lot to be anxious about. The trip down, the ceremony, hotels, traffic, whether we could fit my child's worldly goods into our vehicle, not to mention the emotional impact of my "baby" graduating from college and starting a brand-new life!

I decided from the beginning that I couldn't handle everything on my own, so I went to God and asked him to handle the details for me. The trip, the traffic, the graduation, even fitting all my youngest child's belongings into our vehicle.

Sure enough, our Heavenly Father was faithful. He took care of every single detail. The entire weekend went off without a hitch and we successfully brought the baby of the family, and all of his possessions, back to our hometown.

Are you feeling overwhelmed? Why not ask God to take care of the details? He is not only faithful. He will not only help you, but as we saw in our of our devotionals earlier this week, the Lord will go above and beyond, helping more than we could even imagine!

Coffee With Jesus: The Second Cup

Day Six: Beyond College 2

Scripture: Luke 18:1-8

With graduation taken care of with all the details handled by our Heavenly Father, it was time to focus on the next large issue looming before us: Launching my youngest child into adulthood with a "grown-up" job.

He had previously applied to the company where I worked, and I had thought I might be able to help him by forwarding his resume directly to the hiring manager. Alas, it was too late; the entry-level positions had all been filled

There was a consolation prize, though; there was a slot open for a summer internship. It wasn't quite the job we were hoping for him, but it was full time and a way for my child to get a foot in the door.

As the internship started, so did the prayers. There was an above average chance that if he did well, it could lead to a full-time position. So, I prayed... and I prayed... and then prayed some more. Every day during the internship, I prayed that God would open a door for my child.

The internship passed, my child did well... but there was no offer. Other interns started to see offers... but not him. Then, with only two days left in the internship, my child got the email he had been waiting for all summer; an invitation to apply to a full-time position!

My son got the job! Waiting can be tough, but if you are persistent in your prayers, God will reward that persistence and grant you what you ask. That does not mean God always says, "Yes," but God always looks out for our best interests, and He will always provide for us.

Is there a major life event you are waiting for? Bring it to our Heavenly Father. Be persistent and be patient. God will provide!

Week 6: Above and Beyond

Day Seven: Beyond Victory

Scripture: 1 Corinthians 15:53-58

I shared this earlier, but please bear with me as I share again, for a different reason. One calm evening in Afghanistan, I was at our headquarters and working in our shoddily constructed wood hut we called an office. It was late and I was finishing up a report from my latest round of base inspections in Afghanistan. Then, thanks to Microsoft, I got the "blue screen of death" and lost an hour's worth of work. I was furious! I chucked the pen I was holding across the room and let out an expletive as loud as I could. I quickly found out I was not alone in the building, as a friend of mine came over to inquire what was wrong. Needless to say, I was embarrassed. What should have been nothing more than a slight irritation had sparked blinding fury.

That incident made me aware that I was losing control of my emotions and, coupled with the fact that I had been starting to feel depressed, I realized something bigger must be going on. I sought out a psychologist and was diagnosed with PTSD. I was due to leave Afghanistan soon so the immediate help available was limited. Not wanting to be the stereotypical veteran with PTSD, I hid my condition. I buried it deep and built a façade around me. I fooled a lot of people, but I could not fool God.

One evening, a few months after I returned home, I was at an evening prayer meeting. I don't even remember what we talked about, but I do remember being on my knees, and God breaking down every wall, every façade I had built. All the emotions I had tried to bury came flooding to the surface. I am not ashamed to admit it: I was bawling. The process proved extremely healing. God not only broke down the walls I was trying to hide behind, He not only brought the buried emotions to the surface, He healed me. God restored me. Sometimes, we need to talk to a psychologist or therapist. Sometimes, God intervenes directly.
In this case, I needed both and through my tears, God brought me to victory.

Are you struggling? Bring it to God. Whether it is through therapy or God's healing hand, He WILL bring you to victory!

Week 6 Notes

Week 6: Above and Beyond

Coffee With Jesus: The Second Cup

Week 7: Give it to God

Coffee With Jesus: The Second Cup

"No matter how fierce the storm, no matter how piercing the darkness, God is with us." - Excerpt, Day 2

Week 7: Give it to God

Day One: Coffee to Calm the Nerves

Scripture: Jeremiah 29:11, 22-24, Psalm 37:34, Romans 8:28

Driving in Qatar is unique. The speed limits are strictly enforced, but the Qataris drive WAY over the limit regardless. Many drivers there ignore lines whenever it suits them. Normally, people just cope, but one day on the way to work, I saw firsthand what could happen; I witnessed a single-vehicle accident.

The driver was a member of the Qatar military. He was driving extremely fast and had a tire blowout. That caused him to lose control of his vehicle. After several swerves, he ricocheted from one side of the highway to the other, bouncing off the concrete barricades. His car eventually came to rest near an off ramp. The car itself was messed up badly, The whole front end was pushed in and coolant, oil, and transmission fluid was leaking all over the place, rear lights were busted out and of the front wheels was bent inward. The driver was bleeding when we approached the vehicle.

My coworker called 999 (the local emergency number), and I applied what little first aid I could: basic Ice, Compression, Elevation for the bleeding and ensuring the man stayed awake and alert. Once the police and an ambulance arrived, we made our statements. After ensuring the man was being treated, we left the scene and continued on to work. One thing that struck me as odd is that nobody else stopped. We just happened to be in the exact right place at the exact right time to provide the proper aid.

God's timing is incredible. If we had left a minute sooner or a minute later, or if we had taken a different route, we wouldn't have been there at exactly the right time to render assistance. God's timing is perfect. Sometimes, He puts us where He needs us to help others, and sometimes God brings people to us when we need help. Has God ever put you in just the right place at just the right time?

Coffee With Jesus: The Second Cup

Day Two: How to Recover From Rock Bottom

Scriptures: Jeremiah 17:14; Luke 18:1; Psalm 34:18

Sometimes, we may find ourselves in a situation where we are so beat down and feel so defeated that the only words, we can muster in prayer are, "God, Help!" Honestly, that is all we need to say. God is always with us and He always hears our prayers. When all we can say is, "God, Help!", He hears our prayer and provides us with whatever help we need.

When we are at our absolute lowest, God is at our side. Sometimes, things can seem hopeless. Sometimes, it is hard to see even the thinnest sliver of light in the darkness. However, no matter how fierce the storm, no matter how deep the darkness, God is with us. As Christians, we have that eternal hope. We are heirs to the eternal promise. We just need to seek God and HE will provide for all our needs.

In Christian circles, it is popular to say, "Give it to God!" While that is excellent advice, the *how* is often missing. Exactly HOW do we give it to God? How do we turn things over to Him when we are at rock bottom?

First, please know that God is with you. Second, cry out to our Father. He hears your prayers, no matter how few words you use. If all you can say is, "God, Help!", that's enough. Third, read your Bible. There are scriptures to help you in any situation. Is your problem anger? Psalm 37:8. Is your probably anxiety? Luke 12:20-24.

I can tell you from experience that God will help you, that God is with you. Cry out to Him. Read the Word. His promises are eternal and He promises to help us. No matter what you're going through, no matter what storms you may be facing, God is with you. Our "God is a very present time of trouble." (Psalm 46:1).

Week 7: Give it to God

Day Three: The Bear

Scriptures: Philippians 4:6-7

By the time my middle child had started his senior year of college, he was on his third vehicle inside of a year. The latest vehicle was your typical "beater." It was old, smelly, and held together with spit and duct tape. One evening I received a fateful phone call: The Bear, as the beater was known, had broken down. My child was on the side of the road, in the middle of nowhere. Doing my best not to panic, I asked if he was safe (he was), if the vehicle was out of danger (it was), and what the problem was.

I gave him a few pointers over the phone, but vehicle made a grinding noise and refused to start. I advised him to take an Uber and arrange for the Bear to get towed the next morning. The moment I was finished talking to my child, I called my Father... my Heavenly Father. I started rattling off a list of requests but quickly stopped. I took a deep breath, asked God to be in the details and to please take care of the entire situation.

Two days later, my child had still not had his car towed to a mechanic. I again started to panic. Would the state tow it away as an abandoned vehicle? Would I be slapped with hundreds of dollars in towing and storage fees? Thousands? I quickly stopped myself. I took a deep breath and again brought the situation up to my Heavenly Father. Reassured that He was still in control, even with all the unknowns, I reached out to the local police and was eventually directed to the towing company that had the vehicle. The vehicle was beyond hope. Fortunately, the company that towed it would also junk it. The towing fees and storage fees were covered by the money we'd get for scrapping the car. We were down a vehicle, but not out hundreds, perhaps thousands, of dollars.

I had asked God to handle the situation for me, and He did! Even when I started to panic, He calmed my fear, led me on the correct path, and HE worked out the details in the end. Are you facing a problem where you are unsure how to proceed? Unsure what to do? Bring it to God! Ask him to take care of it for you, and HE will. I know He will, because He did for me.

Coffee With Jesus: The Second Cup

Day Four: Gorilla Tape

Scriptures: Ephesians 6:10-18

What do Mondays, Gorilla Tape, belts and Jesus all have in common?

That seems kind of random, doesn't it?

In talking about the armor of God, the Bible tells us to "stand firm... with the belt of truth buckled around your waist." (Eph 6:14). Back in Paul's day, the belt held all of the armor together. It held up the greaves, held the sword and dagger, and it kept the armor tucked so it would not impede movement.

Jesus declared that HE is the truth (John 14:6). Jesus is the belt that holds everything together. Gorilla tape also holds things together. In fact, I used Gorilla tape to hold my Bible together. At one point, I even used Gorilla tape to hold pieces of my car together!

It may seem a little odd to use Gorilla Tape as a metaphor. After all, Gorilla Tape can, and does, fail whereas Jesus will NEVER fail you. No matter how difficult the circumstances, no matter how relentless the storm, Jesus will hold you together.

When you are stuck in the miry clay of life, our Lord and Savior will pick you up and place your feet firmly on solid ground. Know that Jesus is with you always. Jesus will help you always. No matter what life throws at you, Jesus will be there for you.

Do you feel like your life is falling to pieces? Does it seem like things are coming apart at the seams? Call out to Jesus. He WILL help you.

Jesus will hold everything together!

Week 7: Give it to God

Day Five: Is it OK to be Anxious?

Scriptures: Philippians 4:6-7; 1 Peter 5:6-7

The Bible tells us that we should not worry, that we should not be anxious. Some Christians take this to be a divine command and claim that worrying is a sin. I've felt bad many times for experiencing worry or anxiety.

However, I've discovered that there are some situations where it is OK.

There are many caveats to this revelation. First, the people who tell you that anxiety is a sin are overlooking the real importance of what the Bible says: Bring your worries to God! It is normal and natural to worry or be anxious. Both are very human emotions. The key is to realize that God WILL take care of you. All you have to do is bring your worries to Him and trust Him.

One evening, soon after my little baby (i.e. My youngest child) got a driver's license, the rest of my family and I went out, leaving my youngest alone. With fresh license in hand, the youngest decide to drive to a nearby Taco Bell for dinner; the very first time this child drove solo.

I was at least 45 minutes away and should anything have happened it would have taken a long time to get there to help.

Needless to say, I prayed, and I felt God's comfort. In this case, I also apologized to God for worrying, but the response was not what I expected. It was almost as if God gave a little chuckle and told me it was OK. *"You are worried for your child, and that is normal as a parent."*

I may buck tradition here, but I don't think it's a bad thing to worry or to be anxious. The key is to bring that worry and anxiety to God. Bring our Father the whole situation, and He will take care of it, just like the loving parent He is.

Coffee With Jesus: The Second Cup

Day Six: God's Got This

Scripture: Romans 15:5-8

When my youngest took the road test for his driver's license, I was pretty nervous. OK, I'm not going to lie, I was *very* nervous. It wasn't even about whether he would pass or fail. I wondered, "What if he got into a wreck? What if he hit something, or worse, someone? What if the instructor was a real grouch? What if he had an anxiety attack during the test?"

I was working myself up into a real frenzy, but then I stopped, took a deep breath and prayed. I prayed for protection for my child, and I prayed for peace for both my child and me.

With (an admittedly forced) calmness, I stood and watched as he pulled out and went on his way.

He returned only a few minutes later. I was a little confused. Apparently, the driving test was fairly short and not very difficult. It appeared I was a tougher driving instructor than the examiner was. My child had passed!

No accident, no anxiety attack, no grouchy examiner. The road test itself was relatively simple and my child passed with ease. It made me wonder. I was getting myself all worked up for something that turned out to be no big deal. That was not the only time I have done such a thing.

I realized that even when I am afraid, God's got this. God has *everything* under control.

Is there something in your life that you are worried about? Have a series of 'what ifs' caused you go crazy with anxiety? Give it to God. God will not only take care of things for you, but things may turn out to be much simpler than you have realized.

No matter what you are worried about, give it to our Father. Trust in Him.

God's Got this.

Week 7: Give it to God

Day Seven: Who are You?

Scripture: Matthew 4:1-11

In the 1970s classic Kung Fu movie *Enter the Dragon*, Bruce Lee is challenged to a series of fights. During one fight, Lee's opponent tries to intimidate him by breaking a board. Lee calmly replies, "Boards don't hit back."

That wasn't the reaction his opponent had hoped for. He wanted to taunt Lee into proving his strength and perhaps even find a weakness in the process, but it didn't work. The problem was that Bruce Lee knew he could break a board. There was no need for him to engage in such a petty display. Through his refusal to perform simple tricks, he displayed confidence in who he was.

In a way, this scene is like what happened to Jesus in the wilderness. The devil taunted Him and challenged Him to, "…command this stone to become bread" (Luke 4:3). From one point of view, this might seem like an impressive test of Jesus' power, but when you consider that John 1:3 tells us, "Through him all things were made; without him nothing was made that has been made," it seems as silly as Bruce Lee breaking a board. Jesus knew that he could do it. It wasn't so much a test of Jesus' ability as it was a test of His trust in the Father, so He simply answered, "It is written, 'Man shall not live by bread alone'" (Luke 4:4).

Even though Jesus was tired and hungry in the wilderness, He had complete trust in God. If you know who you are, and you trust in who you belong to (God), then you'll be in a much better position to stand firm against Satan's taunts.

What lie is Satan whispering into your ears? What truth about God can you hold onto?

Week 7 Notes

Week 7: Give it to God

Coffee With Jesus: The Second Cup

Week 8: You Are a Child of God

Week 8: You Are a Child of God

Coffee With Jesus: The Second Cup

"Be like a child and the Kingdom of God will belong to you."
- Excerpt, Day 2

Week 8: You Are a Child of God

Day One: God of Comfort

Scripture: 2 Corinthians 1:3-6

The overarching theme of this devotional book is "Comfort"; God comforting us through our anxieties and through our troubles. I have shared my own trials and anxieties, as well as those of a few of my friends and coworkers, in the hope that you can find comfort the same way that we did: through our Heavenly Father.

Through each and every storm, God is right there with is. There is hope and comfort in this knowledge, but there is also a responsibility we have to our brothers and sisters in Christ. Paul tells us that God, "…comforts us in all our troubles, so that we can comfort those in any trouble with the comfort we ourselves receive from God."

As God carries us through the storms of life, we not only can grow and mature as followers of Christ, but we also gain hope and faith for our next trial, our next storm. When we witness our family in Christ going through similar circumstances, we can share with them that hope that we have gained from our own experiences.

It is my sincere hope that as you have gone through this devotional, you have learned from the experiences that we have shared and that you will lean on the Lord during the trials you will face in life. When have read the devotional all the way through, please feel free to begin again. The lessons are enduring and will remain true.

Even more, I hope that as you grow from your own trials, you will share what you learned to help your fellow Christians. By sharing your own testimony, you can give the same hope and comfort that you have received to others.

Coffee With Jesus: The Second Cup

Day Two: Be Like a Child

Scriptures: Matthew 19:13-15

When my kids were little, I would joke with them a good bit. Sometimes, when the room was dark, I would use a deep booming voice and say, "And Todd said, 'Let there be light!'" and then flip the light switch and the lights would come on.

As kids, they loved it. As teenagers, not so much. As adults they would humor me sometimes, but the childhood wonderment was clearly gone.

There is a deep innocence in being a child. An unconditional acceptance and a desire to be loved or held.

As Christian, we have that. Our Father in Heaven gives us unconditional acceptance and love. Our Father in Heaven holds us when we need it.

Jesus has told us that the Kingdom of Heaven belongs to children. Our Savior is not talking in the literal sense. What he is saying is that He wants us to have that same innocence. He wants us to lean on Him and His Father.

When we are hurt, we should run to our Heavenly Father. When we just want to be held, we should cry out to the Lord. Children rely on their parents to meet their needs. We should rely on our Father to have our needs met.

Be like a child and the Kingdom of God will belong to you.

Week 8: You Are a Child of God

Day Three: Will God Forgive Me?

Scriptures: Luke 15:11-32

My college experience was not quite the "normal" college experience. I spent an entire year at sea in the U.S. Merchant Marine as part of my studies. Typically, the students at my alma mater will cram four years of school into three years and then spend a year at sea on a merchant ship. During my sea year, I did many things that you would expect a sailor to do while in port. It was a different time then, no smart phones, no video cameras everywhere and finding places was mostly through word of mouth. Still, when the ship pulled into port, we would find places and blow off steam from weeks at sea.

I was already a Christian at the time, and I knew that most of what I was doing in port was wrong. I did it anyway. I enjoyed it. I had a good time with my compatriots. I basically told Jesus, "Look, I'm going to go ashore and do things you don't want me to do, so you stay here." Yup. I told the creator of the universe, "I want to have fun, so you can't come." Like the prodigal son Jesus spoke about, I eventually came to my senses. I stopped going to those places and started doing more "tourist stuff" rather than " sailor stuff". My compatriots noticed. Some joined me, some wrote me off. Still, I made a conscious choice to stop despite any repercussions among my friends.

I couldn't ask for forgiveness, though. Although I had stopped sinning, I felt unworthy to go before my creator and even talk to Him, let alone ask for His forgiveness for things I knew were wrong and yet did anyway. Then one day it hit me like a bolt of lightning. I know that sounds like a cliché, but that is the only way to describe the revelation I had:

I WASN'T worthy. That's why Jesus died… for me… while I was still lost in sin. That's how much He loves me. That's how much He loves you! No matter what you do, no matter how badly you have sinned, God will forgive you. Do you feel like a prodigal child? Go to God, ask for His forgiveness. He loves you SO MUCH that He will forgive all of your sin!

Coffee With Jesus: The Second Cup

Day Four: Will God Restore Me?

Scriptures: 1 John 1:8-10

In yesterday's reading, I told you about a period of my life when I knowingly and willfully fell into a life of sin. I shared how I didn't feel worthy of God's forgiveness. I shared how God loves us so much that He will forgive us anyway. No sin is too great for God to forgive.

That is only part of the story, though. My sin was so great, that even after God forgave me, there was a tremendous sense of guilt. My relationship with God suffered. Not because He had forsaken me, but because I had a hard time accepting that I was forgiven. I still felt unworthy to serve him.

That carried that guilt and feeling of unworthiness with me until I returned to school to continue my studies on campus. I tried doing my own quiet time or devotional time and I had trouble. Again, God had not forsaken me, but I had trouble acknowledging His love and forgiveness. That is a consequence of sin that many people don't talk about: the lasting effect even after we are forgiven.

One weekend, a month or two after the term had started, a campus Catholic group sponsored a TEC retreat. TEC stands for Teens (or Twenties) Encounter Christ. Even though I was not Catholic, I asked if I could attend. They were very accepting and happy to have me at the retreat. I remember Saturday night very well, even all these years later. The priest was talking about forgiveness and how when God forgives us, he washes away ALL our sin. It is us, His children, who tend to hold on to it. The priest then handed out a piece of flash paper (this paper leaves no ash behind) and told us to write our sins on it. I filled it up, front and back. I wrote everything I could remember from my time at sea. Then we all put them into a steel pan and the priest lit them on fire. They all vanished! I literally saw the sins that had been weighing me down go up in smoke!

The burden had been lifted! I had been weighed down for so long I actually felt giddy! Not only had God forgiven me, God had RESTORED me! Are you weighed down by sin, even after it's forgiven? Bring it all to God. God will cleanse you from ALL unrighteousness... all your sins will go up in smoke!

Week 8: You Are a Child of God

Day Five: God of Second Chances

Scriptures: Philippians 4:6-7, James 1:2-4

During the early days of COVID, I had given up Facebook for Lent. It really helped my mental health, and the time that I would normally spend scrolling through a seemingly endless newsfeed was spent in prayer and in reading God's Word.

One Sunday, I felt compelled to sign in to Facebook. As Lent is observed six days of the week, Sunday is traditionally a "skip" day, so I thought, OK, sure. Well, I could see there were quite a few people worried about a new disease that was starting to spread. So, I posted a short encouraging message that was well received. I wound up making my Lent about comforting and encouraging people rather than giving up Facebook. Things went well, but then God asked me to step WAY outside my comfort zone.

I felt called to make a short video and post it on Facebook. I told God, "No. Absolutely not. No way, no how, not going to do it." That's right, I told my creator, the one who spoke the universe into existence, "No!" I'm not proud to admit it, but when God called me to serve Him and comfort His people, I balked.

Fortunately, in my case, there were no whales involved (like there was with Jonah). God was actually very patient with me, but He was also very persistent. After about a month, I decided to obey Him and I made a short video. I released it on Facebook and several hundred people watched it. I could tell, right away, that there was this tremendous hunger for comfort among the Body of Christ.

About a month after the video was released, I felt God calling me to start a podcast. This time, I jumped in with both feet. Even though I had told God, "No," before, rather emphatically so, He saw fit to give me a second chance! Our God is a loving God, giving us second, third and fourth chances!

Have you told God, "No" recently? Tell Him, "Yes!" and experience his Love and His grace!

Coffee With Jesus: The Second Cup

Day Six: Did We Miss the Rapture?

Scriptures: 1 Corinthians 15:51-57

I am a little ashamed to admit the sheer length of time it took to write this book. In that time, at least over the year or two prior to me completing the book, there was a lot of talk in various Christian circles about the end times, and about the rapture in particular.

Online content creators were posting videos claiming that, "The end was near" or that the rapture was imminent.

Now, these sorts of predictions have been made since the dawn of time, but with world events being what they were in the 2020's, they found a renewal.

Things came to head one day when an autistic friend of one of my children called me in great fear. He saw a video online that had what sounded like a trumpet call in the distance and the content creator had claimed that was the "last trumpet", i.e. a signal of imminent rapture.

I talked to him for a little while and was able to calm him down and reassure him that the rapture was not occurring and that we were not in the end times. Don't get me wrong, Jesus said that nobody knows the day or the hour. However, there are many unscrupulous types who make false claims and predictions in spite of our Savior's words.

You are a child of the Most High, Living God. One day, our Savior WILL return for us. As Christians we have great hope, if not certain knowledge, that Jesus will return. He said He would, and I firmly believe He will.

Instead of chasing predictions or being afraid of what we see online, let us, as Christians, rejoice in the knowledge that Christ will return for His children. Let us eagerly anticipate the day when we rise up to meet Him in the sky. There will be no more tears, no more suffering, just eternal joy. That is definitely something to be hopeful for!

Week 8: You Are a Child of God

Day Seven: You Matter!

Scriptures: John 1:11-3; Romans 8:37-39

You matter! You are a child of the Most High and Living God!

There is nothing on Earth or the heavens that will ever change that. We are more than conquerors through Christ, and nothing can ever pull us out of our Father's hand.

Throughout this journey, I have shared some of my high points and my low points. I've shared my successes and my failures. Each of those made me who I am today. If there is nothing else you take away from this devotional book, I would like you to at least take this away: You matter!

When we are going through life, it is so easy to get discouraged. It can be all too simple to allow the storms of life to beat us down. When life puts rain and clouds in your path, it is difficult to see the sun. When we are going through hard times, it can be difficult to see THE Son. He is there with us, though. Christ is always by our side.

Why? Because You Matter!

You are a child of God and our Father in Heaven has such an awesome and amazing love for you that He will never, ever leave you, nor forsake you.

No matter what you may be going through, the Lord is with you. You can take anything and everything to Him, and He will help you through your trials. Lost a loved one? God will comfort you. Lost a job? God will provide for you. Sick? God will heal you.

Please allow me to say this one last time: You are a child of the one true God. You Matter!

Coffee With Jesus: The Second Cup

Week 8 Notes

Week 8: You Are a Child of God

Coffee With Jesus: The Second Cup

Week 8: You Are a Child of God

Thank you!

Thank you so much for joining me on this journey! I am so thankful that you have allowed me to join you on yours! My goal is to help and encourage others, whenever and wherever I can. I hope that this book has brought you peace and aided you in your walk with our Heavenly Father.

Please feel free to share these devotionals with friends and family if you feel they will be encouraged by them. If you would like more comfort or more information about Coffee With Jesus, you can learn about us, our mission and our podcast at our website:

https://www.coffeewithjesus.info

If you have thoughts or comments you would like to share you may reach out to us through our website as well.

I pray unceasing blessings upon you as you continue growing in your spiritual walk!

Coffee With Jesus: The Second Cup

www.ingramcontent.com/pod-product-compliance
Lightning Source LLC
Chambersburg PA
CBHW020013050426
42450CB00005B/452